CASHFLOW

&

GROW

BY

TYLER MCBROOM

Ordering Information: Quantity sales. Special discounts are available on quantity purchases by corporations, associations, and others. Orders by U.S. trade bookstores and wholesalers.

www.DreamStartersPublishing.com

Table of Contents

Introduction 4

Why Cash Matters 10

Net Income Matters More than Revenue 20

The Power of a Current and Accurate Set of Books 32

Monitoring Your Top KPIs to Increase Real Cash Profits ... 45

Benchmark Against the Best in Your Industry 57

Where Did All My Cash Go 70

Have a Business Model That Speeds up Cash
as You Grow 81

Cash Reserves to Weather the Economic Downturns 92

Utilize Your CPA for Tax Planning to Lower
Your Largest Expense - Taxes 101

Review Your Financial Terms - Both Length
of Loans and Interest Rates 111

Culture Drives Profitability 118

Social Media Strategies to Grow Your Business 130

Conclusion 138

Introduction

Adopting a Growth Mindset

Are you a business owner who wants to grow to the next level? Do you always seem to look at your tax bill at the end of year and wonder where your money went? Is it time to start thinking differently about how you make financial decisions? If so, then this book is for you.

As a CPA (Certified Public Accountant--but not the boring kind) who works with business owners all around the United States, I will tell you this: every client I have worked with who has achieved lasting success has been obsessed with constantly expanding their mindset and identity. That's where it all begins.

So, I figured it's only appropriate to open this book with this message: **Growth Mindset** is everything.

Through the expansion of my own business (especially in the past few years), I discovered the absolute power of having the right mindset to allow that to happen. Everyone knows me as the TAXSAVER on Instagram, but I didn't start out that way either. Let me explain.

I graduated from college in 2008, just in time for the financial disaster, with a degree in Creative Writing. I had always loved numbers and remember doing math problems in

4

my head just to pass the time during family road trips. But I thought accounting as a career would mean sitting behind a computer and putting numbers in a box, so I ran as far away from that as I could with my studies.

While I was in school, the economy was great and all my professors said employers didn't care what type of degree you had—just that you *had* a degree. I learned the hard way that this rule did not apply during a major recession.

It didn't take long to see that my English degree was not going to get me anywhere—and I got tired of being broke! I went back to school and got my Masters in Business while dabbling in marketing as well.

So, how did I go from a broke creative writing graduate with nothing to my name but a piece of paper to running a multi-million dollar company in just a few short years?

I got serious about improving my mindset.

When I became a partner with my dad in his accounting firm in 2016, he said he didn't want to take a pay cut to bring me on. We sat down and said, "Let's grow this thing!" That was the start of my education in the Growth Mindset. By simply telling ourselves *we had to* grow, we started looking for ways to make that happen.

And we've been rapidly growing ever since, nearly doubling our headcount every year. It's amazing what can happen when you adopt a philosophy, do not compromise, and trust the plan.

We started giving talks to real estate agencies, educating them on our system to increase cashflow and lower taxes significantly. It was a niche that worked right away, and we grew about 50% that year! But the growth mindset didn't go away whatsoever.

In fact, that was when we doubled down on growth and I got serious about social media, hiring someone full time to focus on building my Instagram and Facebook following (more on how that can impact your business later).

Another key change happened when we changed how we identified ourselves with colleagues and other business associates. Whenever I talked about our company, it began with the phrase, "**We are a rapidly growing accounting firm...**"

It might not seem like a big deal to you, but that phrase did wonders for our opportunities and our team's morale. The growth mindset affected every decision we made and served as a compass for the strategic direction for our firm. We always made room for more, even when it felt like we were overflowing.

Once you make the transition from wanting to make a living to wanting to build an empire, everything changes. When we started signing up $25,000 a month in new business, we thought that was amazing. But just a few quick years later we are averaging $300,000 a month in growth and it feels normal!

Success is an inside job, or as Tony Robbins puts it, "*The number one obstacle to the growth of any business is the skills and psychology of the owner.*" It starts with a belief system and becomes a reality. **If you are not committed** to growing your own internal psychology, then you will have a much more difficult time taking action on the important skills you will learn from this book. There is no secret path to growth except through a relentless, consistent commitment to upgrading your internal belief system.

As our firm started to grow, so did my skills in developing relationships. We began to say, "Yes!" to each opportunity that presented itself, and that led me to join a number of business groups to continue expanding my network. Through those networks I learned the skills to really grow my audience, I got connected to the people who knew how to get me on Forbes, and over the next couple years I established some key partnerships that have blown me away. Life was good, and we rolled into 2020 experiencing unprecedented growth.

Then COVID-19 hit.

I watched each week in March as our leads started to plummet at the time of the year where they are normally their highest. Saving on taxes was suddenly no business owner's top priority. Their key concern was keeping their business *in business.*

Instead of retreating, though, we continued to look for growth opportunities and different ways to serve business owners.

That is when we pivoted to help companies with disaster relief and obtaining government PPP loans. It became extremely obvious that businesses needed guidance during this time period. We adjusted the ship, helped businesses survive, and our growth skyrocketed during the early days of COVID-19. As I write this at the end of 2020, we have had our highest annual growth in the company's history.

The COVID-19 experience proved to me that no matter what is happening around you, your brain will show you a way to growth—when you keep the right mindset. It's like when you go to buy a new car, and suddenly you see that car everywhere on the road. Your brain is now AWARE of that type of vehicle, and so you notice it everywhere.

By training your brain to have a growth mindset, it will make you AWARE of the infinite opportunities you have to build a successful business. This journey of running a *rapidly growing CPA firm* has taken me places I would have never imagined, and we still have a long way to go.

But it started with that growth mindset. And was followed by relentlessly adding as much value to our clients and online community as possible.

One final note on mindset: Adopting a growth mindset will help you in bringing revenue *in* the door. Then you must learn how to keep it. If you want a help in increasing your cash flow and lowering your taxes, the pages that follow will provide that roadmap for you. But, make a *Growth Mindset* your obsession first.

This book is for the countless Business Owners out there who are working hard every day to making their own reality, working to "carry their own weather," as the great Stephen Covey says. Entrepreneurs are the backbone of the economy, and I love hearing some of their amazing stories of how they came from nothing and made their dreams come true.

It's immensely satisfying when I am able to play a part in their success. I am a CPA—a Certified Public Accountant—and yet, I've had more than one entrepreneur tell me that our work has literally saved their business. The tools you will learn in this book were the tools we used to do just that. Whether your business is just getting started, experiencing wild growth, or seems on the brink of failure, I am here to tell you that there is ALWAYS a way forward.

Chapter One

Why Cash Matters

Whether you are growing by leaps and bounds in good times, struggling in an economic downturn, or just plugging along, **cash is the life blood of your business**. Once you pull up short on cash, it quickly becomes extremely difficult to dig out of that hole. In fact, over 80% of small businesses that fail, do so because of one thing – failure to properly manage cash flow.

Of course, cash flow is a broad topic that can mean many things. It could be they started up with too little capital, invested in too much inventory, or hired too quickly. Whatever the reason, most otherwise successful business ventures go south, due to mismanaging cash flow.

New business owners are surprised when their venture is growing faster than they imagined, and yet they find themselves in the uncomfortable position of searching for ways to pay the bills. How is that possible? They begin to feel that, no matter how much they grow, the cash will always flow out of the business faster than it comes in. Is the reality of a growing business just that the wheels turn faster and faster without any increase in profit? For many businesses, this is the unfortunate reality—growth drains your cash faster than a stagnant business.

Without a solid understanding of the impact of cash flow on a growth curve, these owners find themselves chasing the dream, but finding it always just out of reach. They are under the illusion that bringing in more revenue is the secret to success, so they risk it all for that goal. They focus on **making** more instead of **keeping** more.

All along, keeping more money is the obvious goal that gets lost in the rush for revenue. They believe that eventually, if they bring in enough revenue, they will make a profit. But revenue alone cannot a rich man make. Too often, the expenses continue to outpace the income, no matter how big you become or how fast you grow.

It takes discipline to manage your growth so that it doesn't outgrow your cash. The temptation to invest in inventory and to add employees clouds the reality of being able to pay for them. *Just sell more stuff and we'll be fine, right?*

It just seems to make sense to go for it and expand as quickly and as much as possible while you can. You will find yourself going further and further out on a ledge to keep the growth coming, believing that increased growth correlates to success. But without disciplined growth and a cash flow plan, you will convince yourself to leverage more and more until you hit the wall.

Cash shortfalls cause business owners to make knee-jerk reactions and poor decisions, where they are forced to give up equity or take on unnecessary debt just to cover the ever-growing, out of control expenses. Growth and revenue can hide the sins you commit in the course of business. But, if you are not always carefully managing your cash, it will catch up to you, sooner or later.

When my company assesses a business, we first look at the annual revenue and compare it to the cash balance. Having $500,000 on hand if you are a $50,000/yr business is outstanding, but having the same $500,000 on hand if you are a $1,000,000,000/yr business indicates you are barely surviving by the skin of your teeth and in danger of failing.

One way of measuring the health of a business is to look at your cash balance in terms of **Days' Sales**, which equals Annual Sales/365. A rule of thumb is that you should have between 60 and 90 days of sales on hand in cash (and even more if your business has more one-time sales than recurring revenue). So, for example, if your annual sales are $1,000,000, then:

$1,000,000/365 = $2,739.73 per day in sales.

Cash on hand should ideally be: $2,739.73 X 90 = $246,575.70

It's easy to see that, in tough times, reserves can save your business from failure; just look at what happened to the businesses that didn't have any reserves to deal with Covid-19. *But growth will dry up your cash too*. New inventory and new employees can quickly drain your reserves when they are not accounted for in your business model. That model needs to be designed for growth—to speed up the cash as you accelerate, not slow it down.

We will discuss tips for managing your cash so you don't find yourself in the position too many businesses do - growing 150% and running out of cash. Cash is what drives your ability to grow wisely; it not only has to be managed properly, it also has to be predicted accurately.

Just like investors in the stock market, many business owners fall into the trap of buying/buying/buying when they are growing, only to focus on selling/selling/selling when revenue starts falling. The key is in understanding that both small business growth and the stock market have seasons of ebb and flow. No business or stock goes up constantly in a straight line, and if that is your expectation, you are in for a shock.

There are business cycles within each small business, depending on many factors, such as the age of the business, for example. The same is true for the greater economy, which normally cycles through highs and lows in a year. There is a reason that spring follows winter and that businesses have times of harvest and times of planting. Understanding the natural flow of your business allows for predicting what's to come and is part of being sustainable in all seasons.

Our business is a perfect example of how growing too quickly can potentially put you at risk.

After joining the firm and making a commitment to growth, we went gang-busters and had an average compounded growth, that means from one year to the next, of over 43% for several years running (Since Covid-19 hit, that number has doubled.). At the end of the year in 2018, we had a reckoning. We were out of cash from hiring like crazy to keep up with the demand and also from increasing our marketing budget. Even with the incredible growth, we found ourselves having to invest capital into the business. If this can happen to an accounting company, it can happen to anybody!

There is a time when, as painful as it seems, the faucet has to be turned down a bit to allow the cash to catch up with the expenses. We sat down and began to implement some of the techniques we will discuss in this book. We've developed processes on how to grow properly, by looking at the cash flow and not just the revenue.

We also tweaked our business model. In the past, we were giving away thousands of dollars in initial services as a way of attracting new customers. We stopped that and instead, incentivized new clients with an upfront payment followed by a flat monthly fee. They get our help with what they need and our commitment to excellent service, and we get a smooth and predictable monthly cash flow, as well as a client who is with us for the long term and not just trying out a free service. It's been a win/win for our business as well as our clients. The quality of our initial work increased since we were actually getting paid for it, and the clients get the security of knowing we have their backs.

As we continue to refine the process, we constantly improve our ability to see our KPIs (Key Performance Indicators) in real time. It's about so much more than cash flow. For example, we keep an eye on average turnaround days (a measure of service) in real time. If that starts to slip, you won't see it in cash flow until it's too late. Then, once that pattern is established, it's hard to turn around.

These days we are sitting right at our target 90 days of cash reserves, and I sleep much better at night. By changing the way we collect money, setting a budget, and monitoring our KPIs in real time, we were able to pivot our business and turn the faucet back up to full. Then, when COVID-19 hit, we saw what was happening and were able to pivot again.

We saw our volume of new business drop for two consecutive months, which hadn't happened during tax season (harvest time) for several years, until we were able to adjust. By jumping on the government's PPP (Payroll Protection Program) loans, and showing others how to do the same, we not only returned to our prior numbers, we far exceeded them. We are now at an all-time high and project continued growth throughout the year.

The hardship of the pandemic allowed me to see opportunities that I didn't know were out there and success exposed our weaknesses. Getting kicked in the teeth and, essentially, almost failing twice, allowed us to grow bigger each time and in new and more creative ways.

I find most good, strong business owners have all been kicked in the teeth once or twice. They know what failure feels like and that knowledge makes them stronger and better able to pivot when adversity hits. The businesses that never experienced hardship were the ones that failed this year

(2020 during Covid). They were comfortable living on that edge, having no reserve and thinking they would grow forever.

Then, lending tightened up, right when businesses needed cash. Lenders were only willing to lend to those businesses that had cash in the bank, not the ones with revenue but no cash. So, the virus forced businesses to change and adapt, or fail. If they didn't know how to pivot, they lost.

Success and adversity, two sides of the same coin, teach the identical lesson - having cash on hand - not in inventory, not in accounts receivable – will literally save your business and allow you options to pivot when you find yourself facing either side of the coin.

MEASURING RESULTS

How are you currently managing your cash flow?

_____

_____

_____

_____

How can you improve it?

_____

_____

_____

_____

"For better or worse, cash is the oxygen of your business, and you can't last long in any environment without it."

Neil Blumenthal

A Professional Accounting Corporation

Chapter Two

Net Income Matters More than Revenue

Adversity teaches us lessons that make us stronger. This quote from a book I read recently, "The Biggest Bluff" sums this up perfectly:

"Mike Tyson said it best. 'Everyone has a plan until you get punched in the mouth.' And he's right. Until you go through a month of everything going wrong, you won't know whether you have what it takes. You will never learn how to play good poker if you get lucky—it's as simple as that. You just won't."

Maria Konnikova, The Biggest Bluff: How I Learned to Pay Attention, Master Myself, and Win

Konnikova talks about failure in her book and the value it taught her, in poker, but especially in life. She talks about the benefit of failure as "an objectivity that success simply can't offer." When you are able to look objectively at your business, at the numbers and the KPIs without all the emotion and ego attached to it, that is when you start to see the failures as lessons that can signal the way forward.

It all starts with letting go of always wanting to be seen as the winner, always putting the biggest numbers forward to prove you are a success. Numbers don't have emotions, but they tell a powerful story if you allow them to unfold in front of you. Don't be afraid to listen to the story they are telling you and to learn from it.

There are many potential clients that balk at the idea of keeping stats and budgets and finding their blind spots - all the things I talk about with new clients. They say they are too busy to bother with all that cash flow stuff; they are the deal makers, the growers. They are the ones that believe rapid growth is all that matters and the one stat they track is revenue. I never try to convince anyone to work with me. I'm too busy for that!

Keeping your stats is like doing exercise every day. If you think you're too busy or too important to exercise every day, then don't. But you'll be dead sooner than the rest of us who took the time to develop the habits for success, in business and in life.

"Revenue is vanity, profit is sanity, and cash is king."
Verne Harnish from Scaling Up

Whenever I go to any conferences, there is the inevitable bragging that starts amongst the business owners; "I pulled in seven figures last year!", "I grew 50%!", "I hired 30 new employees." You know what they say about a guy that brags too much about the size of his company, right? I call revenue and number of employees, the ego metrics, because they are an easy measure to brag about to hide the truth about your business. If you hired 30 new people in a year, but your revenue only went up $21,000, then you are looking at an intake of only $7,000 per new employee, in other words, a net loss.

Whenever someone brags about their company growing, it's always that TOP LINE REVENUE number...many times that person is drowning in expenses and debt. Revenue growth is important, but even more important is that you make a PROFIT on that revenue.

So, don't get me wrong! Revenue is important! It's exciting and energizing to see that number go up each month, and at the start of a business, it's essential. When we first started, I remember celebrating when our revenue went up by 50% and our net income went up by 100% at the same time. That is not uncommon with a start-up. But, very soon in the life of a new business, other metrics are just as important if not more so. This happens earlier than many realize, I would say when you reach around $200,000 or above. Once you have enough revenue to feed yourself, it's time to focus on building a profitable company.

It's always important to look at the metrics, but at that point in your growth, it becomes essential. At the end of the month, we complete all of our financial reports and KPI analysis so that we can sit down and look at them by the 10th of the next month. Many new business owners mistake their personal income for company profit. They have to remember that they are not the company. So, to get a bottom-line profit number, you have to look at revenue minus expenses, taxes AND the salary you are paying yourself. That is the true profit of the company.

We sat down with one client, a realtor, who told us he was making $300,000 a year. But, once we accounted for all of the expenses of things like travel, taxes, and marketing, he was actually making just under $90,000. That is a very different number than the first one! It's a nice stroke of the ego to say you are making $200,000 or $300,000 a year, but if you start spending as if that's your income when it's not, then you'll get in real trouble very quickly.

For business owners who have employees, it's even more important to get honest with the true profit they are generating in the business. Otherwise, they may find themselves unable to cover payroll one month, and then, their ignorance and denial are affecting families other than their own. The employees did their job in good faith and are now facing a financial catastrophe due to the owner's reckless management of the company.

In my experience, an industry where I see this example played out all too often is with medical practitioners. It makes sense since their education is so focused on the medicinal aspect of the business. They almost like to ignore the financial aspect of the business because they don't want to look at their clients in terms of numbers or money. Many of the patients will have insurance, but just as many won't. So, the doctors will often hire a front-end manager to handle the business side of things and then go about doing what they were trained to do—help patients.

Then they see top-line revenue go up because they are helping more patients! The trouble is that they are focused on that top-line number and never take the time to dive deep into expenses and ways to make the business sustainable. So, the doctors work twice as hard, have even less time to look at the numbers and find themselves making less and less profit as they burn-out from overworking. They chose to have their own practice, so they could have the "freedom" to practice as they choose, without the restrictions of a large company dictating to them. Instead, they become trapped in a quagmire of financial stress.

If they can't run a smooth business, it will inevitably interfere with their ability to take proper care of their patients. I recently read that thousands of independent medical practices are closing their doors this year due to Covid-19. I can't help but wonder how many had the equivalent of 60 to 90 days' sales in cash on hand, or if some of the closures could have been avoided with better cash-flow management?

One of our medical practitioner clients told us that he had no trouble raising revenue. What kept him up at night was that gnawing feeling that his profit margin was not what it should be. He felt his employees didn't have any understanding of the fact that discounting products 20% for his clients was eating into his ability to make more money. There was a disconnect. They saw all the money coming in every day, but didn't understand all the expenses involved in running a practice; heck, just the malpractice insurance alone was over $100,000 a year.

When we sat down and started to review his processes, we saw that all of his incentives and bonus systems in place for his employees were based on top-line revenue. There were no checks in place for expenses. His employees did all the purchases for medical products and office supplies and had no eye towards finding the best deals.

But the more important numbers were not even in the mix; the net income, cost of goods sold, labor percentages, and revenue per full-time equivalent employee. We looked at those numbers and more. He also was collecting a lot of money upfront in terms of prepayments. This is great for cash-on-hand, but can become a liability when you start to consider how much time you owe to your clients and how that interferes with new business.

Once we analyzed his net income percentages, it was clear that his concerns were justified. He needed to be 10% more profitable just to be AVERAGE. He could have an instant raise by closing the place and getting a job with a large medical group. But, once we adjusted pricing, and set budgets, along with a 90-degree change of mindset, his profit margins began improving.

Once we began to get the metrics in place, there was an almost instant relief of stress. Knowing where you are in your business, whether you have a dumpster fire on your hands or are holding your own, gives you a starting point. We started seeing a consistent increase in our doctor's profit line after about three months.

A common question we hear new clients ask is, "Where does the money go?" They know they are pulling in a good amount, but they don't feel it. They forget about the vacation to the Caribbean or the large debt they paid off. They don't look at the accounts receivable that is creeping up until clients may owe them $50 - $100,000. They count that as income and never consider the expense of collecting it, or even the likelihood of having to write it off as time goes on.

By having a laser focus on the bottom line instead of the top line, you are no longer flying by the seat of your pants and buying equipment and supplies without really knowing if you can afford them. A good set of books gives you an ability to make an objective decision about those purchases. You begin to understand not only if you should invest in certain products, but when and how to best pay for them.

It's like investing in the stock market on a hunch instead of studying a stock portfolio and waiting for a good time to purchase. Having a person who is an expert in stocks also helps. We can't all be good at everything. Most business owners were excellent at what they did by trade, and decided they wanted to be self-employed—just because you are a great doctor does not make you a great business operator or suddenly give you the ability to manage your finances.

These folks don't know what a profit and loss statement is, or how to look at any monthly statements with an educated eye. They usually never look at any monthly statements and rely on an accountant to "do their books" at the end of the year to find out how much they made. When it's time to consider a purchase, they will often open their bank account and look at the amount in the checking account to see if they should buy it.

If you are that industry expert who opened a business without a business background, getting a good accounting firm in your corner is going to be critical for success. By a good firm, I mean one that educates you in terms of how to look at the monthly numbers and make sense of them. We initially have to spend more time with new clients to establish that relationship and align our activities with their business goals. But, as time goes on and our new procedures and processes are in place, we can see them less. We teach them how to read the monthly statements and make the necessary adjustments on their own.

It's more than just being hyper-focused on expenses. Most owners don't focus on the right expenses. For example, my dad once became irate that our front staff person had paid $5 for a bottle of Dr. Pepper, so he decided to take a few hours off to go to Costco and get the 30-pack for just $12. He didn't take the time to consider how much his time is worth when he's in the office and not off shopping in the middle of the day! (Sorry, Dad!).

The expenses that really move the needle, like total labor costs, product costs and other areas that really *drive* profitability, are where you should be obsessing over and spending most of your time.

There are no shortcuts—if you want to know what your bottom-line profit is, you are going to have to keep track of your numbers. Not only do your books need to be up to date, they need to be accurate. And that is what we will discuss next.

MEASURING RESULTS

What lessons have you learned from adversity?

_____

_____

_____

_____

How can you continue to learn from it?

_____

_____

_____

_____

"Profit is like oxygen, food, water, and blood for the body; they are not the point of life, but without them, there is no life."

Jim Collins

A Professional Accounting Corporation

Chapter Three

The Power of a Current and Accurate Set of Books

If you own a business, you need *current* and *accurate* financials to make decisions with. It's as simple as that. But not nearly enough business owners practice this habit.

Recently, our company learned the power of accurate numbers again, when we sat down and calculated another metric that is easy to ignore: Client Acquisition Cost, which is how much it costs to get a new client. I thought I had a good handle on that, but hadn't really done the math.

I knew the average value of each client, which is the Client Lifetime Value. Each of our clients spends an average of $10,000/yr on our services and stays with us for approximately 8 years. So, a new client is worth $80,000 to our firm. I figured we spent about $400-500 in marketing costs to acquire each one. But once we did the math and included all the resources involved in signing a new client, things looked a bit different.

We looked at our marketing costs, the costs associated with our sales staff and then even the time my dad and I personally took away from daily business to woo new clients. When all was said and done, the average cost for each new client was around $3000 - 4000! We were off by a factor of 10!

So, in order to get an accurate net Lifetime Value, we needed to subtract the acquisition expense from the $80,000. It's still well worth it to spend that money on getting new client relationships, but knowing the accurate number allows us to make more informed decisions. How many new clients can we afford at this time? This information allows me to look at our growth in terms of expense as well as income. Not knowing this number is one reason that businesses can run into trouble when they grow too fast.

This is the power of good books. You can work on the strategic issues of your business much more effectively with an accurate set of financial metrics. Having current, accurate financials is also the first step in making the transition from business operator to business owner. Without them, it is very difficult to get to a place where you truly OWN your company instead of simply having a job there. Having clear numbers and tracking your metrics gives you the ability to fine tune and elevate your company. When the guessing is over, your confidence will explode.

You'll be looking objectively at the business, not relying "on your gut," which is really another way of saying that you are just rolling the dice and hoping Lady Luck blesses you this quarter. You may win big, but you may go on a losing streak too. Who knows? If you are running your business without a good set of books, no one does.

Even with everything in place; good books, cash on hand, increasing revenue, something can still happen to ruin you. All you can do is increase your odds of success. We know already that even with a great concept, you have an 80% chance of failure if you don't have a handle on cash flow. Do you feel good about those odds? Business ownership is a risky venture and not for the faint of heart. By decreasing your odds of failure due to cash flow issues, you are setting yourself up to go all in. And good cash flow planning requires good books.

How frustrating would it be for you to fail in the face of increasing revenue? Talk about a kick in the teeth! That is one life-lesson that you could possibly avoid by heeding some of the advice I am sharing with you.

We often hear about the importance of working on the business instead of in the business. It's the difference between owning a job versus owning a business. If you are working just to pay yourself a salary and the company isn't generating any excess profits, you simply own a job. But it's a job with a lot of baggage and responsibility.

You have to do all the work of ownership without any of the benefits. Why not go out and get a "real job" in that case? There is something to be said for leaving all the worries of the job there when you go home. There is no advantage to owning a job that you have to take home with you and be responsible for 24/7.

Once you begin really owning your business and knowing your numbers, it becomes easier to steer it in the direction of your dreams. You will know when to apply the brakes, when to pivot, when to hire, and when to go big with inventory and investments. The knowing gives you that ability. You'll start to work smart instead of running around in a whirlwind, trying to keep the business from crashing and burning.

Current AND Accurate

And yet, most business owners feel that the bookkeeping process is just a chore that needs to be done once per year during tax time. So, they gather their bank statements and head over to the accountant's office, usually after getting an extension for their returns. Now we are in July, trying to get a handle on the prior year's numbers. The numbers have lost their power by then. It's like a doctor looking at your blood pressure numbers and blood work from the prior year and trying to adjust your medication.

Good books have to be current and assessed in real time to give you that ability to steer the business properly by making good decisions. But, as they say about computers: "Garbage In, Garbage Out." If your data is not accurate, it's not going to be very helpful.

Just imagine that you are a pilot and you jump in your plane with no flight plan and no dashboard. You might believe you are heading to Miami for a frolic on the beach, but with bad data, you will just as likely end up in New York in the winter. Not only will you be way off course, you'll be terribly underdressed as well! Who is going to want to join you on that plane?

In business terms that means you don't know where the business is headed and what you'll need to have in place when you get wherever it is you are going. You are flying blind, by the skin of your teeth and your odds of crashing are astronomical.

Besides increasing your odds of staying in business, having accurate numbers is also the first and best thing you can do to decrease your tax bill. It will give you the ability to accurately assess your deductions. Without the hard numbers, most business owners tend to under-estimate their deductions. But, even with a low estimate, in the event of an audit, if you can't prove it, it didn't happen.

One of our clients had previously done his tax returns by the "All Expenses End in Three Zeros" method. In other words, he estimated all of his expenses. "I think I spent around $3,000 on my car...and probably about $5,000 on office expenses..."

When he started with our program, he was initially resistant to cleaning up his books; he thought he knew how much he was spending and didn't want to waste time playing with numbers. But, once we got him on board with keeping current and accurate books, he saw the power in the numbers. With the same revenue as the year before, his tax bill was $20,000 less! We saved him that much, not with some complicated tax strategy, but just by making him do his books.

But, it's more than just putting in the data, it also must be reconciled with your bank statement. The bank statements are the way to prove your numbers are accurate. Reconciling your bank statements will not only assure good numbers, it's also the best way to catch fraud and theft, which, unfortunately, happens more than you think.

Most businesses use QuickBooks and have an employee on staff who is writing the checks and manually entering them into the system. Once, we were looking at a client's books and saw two payments that were made out to our firm. The trouble was that we had only received one check! When we pulled the bank statements and looked at the copies of the checks, we found that the check number that was assigned to our firm was written out to one of their employees. She had written the check to herself and posted it in QuickBooks as a payment to our firm.

This happens all the time. Employees see all the income, but none of the expenses. If they have economic stress at home, there is always a temptation to skim a bit off the top. They figure you can afford it, and they need it more than you do. That particular client had over $20,000 taken, and he was only making around $200,000 at the time. If you don't have the books up-to-date and reconciled it's far too easy to have happen to you.

There are a few ways to prevent this scenario. The best way to do this is to reconcile your books with your bank statement each month. Most on-line accounting systems allow you to link up your bank account so this is a fairly simple process. Once you do this, it's easy to see if a check doesn't match what your books list. I may be biased here, but if you feel at all overwhelmed with this task, then it's best for your accountant to reconcile your books each month. Then they will send a discrepancy report for you to review. You may see that you have duplicated an expense, for example, and this can be quickly corrected.

Another important task that can be done easily each day is to immediately put expenses into the appropriate category. Don't wait until it's become an enormous time-consuming task—break it into small steps. I recommend first thing in the morning with your coffee, or at the end of the day with your glass of wine, whichever liquid habit you prefer and would make the task easier for you. It should only take a few minutes.

This step allows you to be current with your numbers. You'll be able to quickly see if you're going over your budget in a particular category and adjust accordingly, in real time. This is not simply an exercise in organizational skills, it means the difference between success or failure.

The categories in your books are like the instruments on your plane's dashboard. Your dashboard may say you have enough gas to get to Miami, but it's not a useful number if it's not accurate and you run out of gas when you're halfway there. The categories are only useful if they are up to date *and* accurate. Only then can you see if you are on track with your budget or overspending without knowing it.

Doing this task regularly will keep you current and then reconciling each month will ensure accuracy. Without both, you'll be flying blind. You may feel confident in making decisions, but they could potentially be the wrong decisions for your business.

We get so many prospective clients calling with the same question, "What is the number one thing I can do to lower my tax bill?" They want some quick and easy trick, like paying their spouse as an employee or writing off travel as an expense. There are some quick things that can help, but my answer will always be the same, "Keep accurate and current books." As you see earlier with the example of the client who saved $20,000 in tax on the same revenue, that is what's going to lower your tax bill more than any other single thing you can do.

On top of keeping your books up to date, proper documentation of expenses is critical. Everything is a deduction until you get audited, then only the expenses you can prove will be allowed. The easiest way to accomplish this is to take a picture of each receipt the moment you get it. There are a number of tools out there for this, and one of our favorites is an app called Divvy. We use Divvy because, in addition to easily storing receipts, it also allows us to give various employees a virtual credit card that has a budget associated with it. Then when you get your statements from the bank, you can easily check the receipts while simultaneously placing budget limits.

We also recommend that you have a business bank account and credit card that is totally separate from your personal account and card. When you go to the store, separate the personal items from the business items and pay for them with the appropriate card. So, when you are in Target and you pick up some new socks and undies along with a printer cartridge and some paper, pay for your personal items with your personal debit card and the business items with the business account. When you get the receipt for the business, take a picture. When you get home and have your glass of wine, categorize them in QuickBooks.

One of the first things an auditor will look at are your receipts from Big Box stores, and you better have them handy. They will line the receipts up with the items in your books and look for personal purchases hidden in there. If you have a receipt from Target for $100 that is listed under Office Supplies, but there is only $25 for printer cartridges and the rest is a video game and a case of beer, they are going to find that very quickly.

But it is also just as likely that there are business expenses on your personal account that you are missing. Be sure to look for things like cell phone, gas, car expenses and travel, that may all be deductible and could be paid for from your business.

What we commonly see in small businesses is an owner using Excel to try to track expenses and payments. The trouble is that it's impossible to reconcile in Excel and you have a huge chance of having errors. Even worse than that, some owners will pencil in categories right on their bank statements and expect an accountant to sort that all out.

The days of showing up at the accountant's office with a shoebox of receipts and your stack of bank statements is long gone. You might be able to do that in the good times when things are booming. But, during the down swings, if you don't have your house in order, you'll be another statistic of a failed small business. You can take your shoebox with you and go home.

MEASURING RESULTS

How current are your books and numbers?

_____

_____

_____

_____

What habit can you add to your daily or weekly routine to improve how you work with your books in your business?

_____

_____

_____

_____

"Money often costs too much. "

Ralph Waldo Emerson

Chapter Four

Monitoring Your Top KPIs to Increase Real Cash Profits

Do you know what your top KPIs (Key Performance Indicators) are? Each business will have 3-5 top metrics that ultimately drive the business towards success. If you obsess over monitoring those primary KPIs in real time, you will maximize your profits, it's that simple.

We've talked about the dashboard on a plane demonstrating the critical numbers to the pilot, let's break that down. At a glance, they can see their speed, the amount of fuel, the altitude, the direction, and the weather indicators, for starters. Those are the indicators the pilot needs to reach the target destination (read: your business goal) at the proper time. If he takes the long way, he may run out of gas. If he is even one degree off in latitude, he will miss his target. If he's too high, he may get too close to another plane. If he is flying into headwinds, he'll use more gas.

For a business, it's the same thing. The owner wants to be able to see the indicators, at a glance, that will drive the business towards its goal. Once you identify your KPIs, then you have to monitor, measure and obsess about them. For example, if you are a chiropractor, you would monitor, among other metrics, the Average Number of Visits per Year across your client list. If you were seeing new patients like crazy, but they were only staying for 2-3 visits, that would help you understand that patient satisfaction was a problem.

If you were only looking at the Amount Collected in a Week, you may not notice the patient satisfaction problem quickly enough. The new patients coming into the office would keep the collections high, but you would not be able to maintain that amount over time or you would be spending more than necessary on marketing for new clients instead of focusing on reducing churn.

Leading vs Lagging Indicators

The Number of Visits per Client would be considered a leading indicator, where the collections are a lagging indicator. When you are considering which indicators to keep tabs on, it's important that the leading indicators are given priority. Most of the "ego metrics" happen to be lagging indicators. But they are also the ones that most business owners love to focus on.

Revenue is a lagging indicator, it may look great all by itself, but without tracking other indicators it can be very deceptive, as we've discussed. For example, if a restaurant is maintaining a certain level of revenue each week, they may think things are great, until they realize that their marketing budget has ballooned to triple what it was and yet, they are not seeing an increase in business.

Here is a secret. If all you do in your business is start to track your KPIs, you will do better than most of your competition. It provides knowledge that changes you and how you manage. Even if you don't think it does, it will. If that chiropractor focused obsessively on the average number of visits per client, he would become acutely aware of making his patients happy with his care.

Let's look at weight loss as an example. The lagging indicator would be your actual weight that starts to change only after you adjust several other factors, such as calories in and exercise duration. If a person wanted to lose weight but the only thing they did to "change" was to step on the scale occasionally, it's likely they won't see results as fast as someone who tracked every calorie.

To use my own business as an example, it really has a few components to it that are quite simple to break down and quantify. First, we have to sell our service, then we have to do the work we promised clients we'd do. From there we have to collect the money and, of course, keep the clients happy, so they will return. Each of these areas of our business have specific metrics for us to track.

For selling, we look at our leads coming in and number of new appointments—which are leading indicators for new proposals signed and ultimately revenue generated. But, if we are not keeping up with doing the work, then using those indicators is going to give us a false metric of the health of the business. We may be selling the service, but taking longer and longer to complete the tasks. So, a good metric for monitoring, alongside the sales metrics, is turn-around time for services. Our turn-around time might increase and that would tell us that we have a problem before the revenue numbers change.

Now, if we are focusing on getting the work done, we may knock it out of the park in turn-around time and in increasing client base, but, if our accounts receivable is going through the roof, then all our efficient work is not getting converted into cash profits. This has happened to us when we were so focused on selling and getting the jobs completed that our accounts receivable went up to $400,000! The longer that sticks around, the more it will cost to collect and the less likely it will get collected in full.

So, as you can see, each stage in the client cycle has its own metrics and is dependent on other components of the business. For you to have a healthy business that is reaching the ultimate goal of PROFIT and CASH in the bank, then you have to develop leading metrics for each aspect of your business.

Once you do this, you will be amazed at how you find yourself focusing on the right things, then seeing your stress levels plummet. You will become proactive instead of reactive. Few business owners get to this point. But, then again, most will fail in the first five years. This is another key reason why!

When a business owner is in reactive mode, he is circling the runway, focusing on the lagging or ego indicators and missing the landing! The only way to become a proactive business owner is to have a good, strong dashboard that you can read in real time. The dashboard should be customized for your specific business and cover its major components. It's really not as complicated as it sounds and the rewards are priceless.

Fathom is one great program we use for this measurement process that provides you with a visual "dashboard" of your finances and syncs easily with your accounting software. It's easy to use, and has great reports and tools to help you assess your business and monitor trends. It's very inexpensive and helps you see your stats quickly and easily.

As you may have noticed, some of the most important metrics are not related to the financial side of the business. In our business, we measure what's called the Net Promoter Score, which is a measure of the loyalty of our clients. It's a simple anonymous questionnaire that asks, "On a scale of 1-10, how likely are you to refer a colleague to our company?" It may be a simple question but it speaks volumes about the future of your company. Here's how it's scored.

A person that marks a 9 or 10 in likelihood to recommend you and your company is called a promoter. They are your bread and butter. Word of mouth referrals are the cheapest way to get a new client and those clients are more likely to be both loyal and to refer others to you. You can't ask for any better than that! They are your ambassadors out in the world, working gratis to spread the good word about you. No business, big or small, would survive without promoters.

The people that score between 0-6 are called detractors. They are unlikely to recommend you and may even discourage others from working with you. They will leave as soon as they can. Your goal is to have very few detractors. The ones sitting right in the middle at 7-8 are considered passives. They may stay with you but are not particularly loyal and could be easily stolen away by a competitor. As sales expert Jeffrey Gitomer said: "Ask yourself a question, do you want your spouse merely satisfied with you or do you want them to be loyal?" You should feel the same way about your clients!

To give yourself a Net Promoter Score, take the total percent of promoters minus the percent of detractors. A score above 50 is considered world class, and a "good" score is anything above zero. If it comes in negative, then you have some serious service issues in your business.

There are so many other ways to look at these numbers and I encourage you to research this powerful tool and use it in your company. Just using this single tool can open your eyes to what is really happening in your business. We not only give this survey to our clients, we give a similar questionnaire to our employees to measure their loyalty to the business as well. The question we ask our employees is, "Would you recommend a job with us to a friend?"

I believe that my employees come first, before my clients. I want to keep them, not just happy, but dedicated and loyal to the company. In addition to looking at the employee NPS (Net Promoter Score), we also track employee turn-over and regularly compare our pay scale to the standard in the industry.

The work we are talking about here is the grunt work. It's not glamorous, it can be tedious and boring. If you are in sales, for example, a leading indicator might be the number of phone calls you make or e-mails you respond to every day, and then what percent were successful. If phone calls are killing it over emails, then you might decide to spend more time there. Are you sending thank-you notes to your new clients? All of the little things make a huge difference.

Whatever your indicator is, phone calls, cards, e-mails, you have to find a way to track its success or you have no idea whether it's worth your time. By getting your financials up to date, you are keeping your dashboard current. A bookkeeper may not be interested in many of these KPIs, they are there to balance your books. But a CFO is looking at all of those numbers. They are looking forward, while a bookkeeper is looking back. That is the kind of work we do for our clients.

Many clients first ask, "How many KPIs should we have?" Well, that depends on your business. If you are a small business, just starting out, you may be fine with 3 good leading indicators. As you grow, it helps to break them down by department. The sales department should have their own three indicators, as should each other department, and each employee should have their own personal KPIs. Usually, three to five KPIs per department tells you what you need to know to pivot and adapt quickly.

To find the best KPIs for you, start with whatever it is that keeps you up at night, then find a way to track it. It may be bills, or it may be that you have grown so much that you are now removed from your clients and want to take the pulse of the business. There are ways to track both. So, what keeps you up at night?

Also, service business is going to have different KPIs than a product-based business. The product-based business is going to be monitoring inventory closely, while the service-based business is more interested in work-in-progress - what they have unfinished in the pipeline. They will be always looking for ways to speed up their processes, while a product-based business will want to minimize the time they hold on to inventory.

Once you master the monitoring aspects and the KPIs begin to show you your business's performance in real time, you can really start to have some fun with your business and fine-tune it in ways you never thought possible. Now you can begin to ask yourself, for example, if it's possible to raise prices, lose some clients, but still increase your profitability. Then you can work less and make more per client. That is just one small example of the ways these numbers will begin to work for you.

So, remember. The KPIs have to be current, leading and customized for your business. You should have a combination of financial and non-financial indicators, and most importantly, you need to look at them and obsess about them regularly! I've included a list of common KPIs below to help inspire you. Get your books current and accurate, find a few leading indicators to monitor, and watch your business take off.

Most Common KPIs

- Net income as a percent of revenue (Net Income / Revenue)
- Revenue per employee (Annual revenue / number of Full-Time Equivalent employees)
- Days Sales in Inventory (Annual Revenue / 365 / inventory balance)
- Days Sales in Accounts Receivable or Payable (Annual Revenue / 365 / AR or AP balance)
- Days Sales in Cash (Annual Revenue / 365 / cash balance)
- Liabilities-to-Assets Ratio: Total Liabilities / Total Assets
- Year over year revenue growth (last 12 month's revenue / prior 12 months revenue)
- Year over year profit growth (last 12 month's profit / prior 12 months profit)

MEASURING RESULTS

List and discuss your top KPIs.

"It's how you deal with failure that determines how you achieve success."

David Feherty

Chapter Five

Benchmark Against the Best in Your Industry

Once you've gotten your books current and chosen your metrics, now what? How can you be sure you are at peak performance and you are competitive? This is when you take a look at others in your industry to see what others are doing on average. What is the typical benchmark for annual growth in your industry? How about the pay scale, or the number of employees? It's one thing to look at your own numbers and hope you have good targets, but even better to set your goals compared to your best competitors.

Your metrics may be different from the industry average, and that might be ok, but it is still critical to at least compare. For example, when we started to look at our accounts receivable (A/R) numbers, we found out that the industry average of Days of Sales in A/R was 60 days and the best in our industry were at 10 days. We were averaging 120 days. Red alert! That number was not OK! We knew we were slow to collect, but didn't realize how bad the problem was until we did the research. We were just cruising along, never knowing it was a bottleneck to cash flow until we compared ourselves to others in the same business.

But, on the other hand, we spend way more for marketing and growth than our competitors, and we are perfectly happy with that. The reason? The benchmark for average annual growth in our industry is 4.4% a year. We are sitting at 70% growth. I am happy to spend more on marketing for an amazing growth rate. Our labor costs are also higher. But we value our employees and don't grind them down during tax season.

Run your metrics against the best and then decide what matters for you. If you find that you are underperforming in certain areas, it will help you focus on what is important. It will confirm your choice of KPIs. Maybe you will see an area of weakness that you never knew existed before.

Each business has a code for the IRS, and they also look at benchmarks. If you are an outlier in a certain metric, it may trigger a red flag for a possible audit. Knowing the industry average is helpful for that reason as well. For example, if a real estate agent puts 30,000 miles on their car in a year that is pretty typical for the industry and that amount of expense wouldn't raise a flag. But if a computer programmer put the same 30,000 miles of auto expense it would definitely trigger an audit flag—not too many computer programmers I know are on the road every day. That being said, if you *do* have more expenses than your industry average, just make sure you can document it (see chapter 3, The Power of a Current and Accurate Set of Books, for more on documentation).

Not all industries will have these benchmarks available, but most do. Usually, you can purchase them for a few hundred dollars each year. We have one client who teaches a drone piloting course. There are no benchmarks for comparison in this niche of an industry—yet. But as it grows, I am sure those numbers will come. Other clients may be able to find their benchmarks for free with Google. We have a tool that shows the benchmarks for most major industries, so we can provide that service to our clients.

One of the indicators the benchmarks will show you is the average percent of revenue a certain category of expenses is, such as the average % of revenue for wages or supplies. If you see that 40% of your revenue goes to rent, and the industry average is 20%, you may want to consider looking for a more affordable space. But, if it's a matter of a bit more in office supplies, don't worry about it; focus and obsess on the things that are going to make the biggest difference in your profit margin.

If your prices are way below average, this tells you that you will probably be able to raise them without losing many clients. Maybe you are holding way more inventory than most, then you have to dig deeper and figure out why.

As an example: My mom has a boutique children's clothing store. She always had the store fully stocked and everyone loved the great selection. But, at the end of each year, she found herself deeply discounting her product to move out old inventory. We decided to look at her industry benchmarks.

She was a small shop, so it's important that we didn't want to compare her to Walmart or huge national chains. When you are looking at these averages, it's important to look at companies who are a similar size to yours. A much larger company has different benchmarks because they have much more leverage when it comes to buying inventory.

We discovered that she was carrying $50,000 more inventory than comparable stores. She usually does her purchases on a quarterly basis, so we worked out a budget for the next cycle that would put her more in line with her competitors, and when she went to buy her inventory, she stuck to her budget. By reducing her inventory, she had $50,000 more cash in the bank. Then, at the end of the cycle, she didn't have to discount as many of her products, so she ended up with increased profit of another $50,000.

This is the power of a good dashboard that is in sync with your industry. Her cash flow increased by $100,000 just by tweaking her inventory and sticking to a budget. Going forward, she will closely monitor her amount of inventory, as well as the number of days the inventory is held.

My mom didn't know what her average amount of inventory should be. The market had already figured that out for her, so she just had to look up the numbers. The same was true for our company, but it was in terms of A/R instead of inventory. We are a serviced-based company so the important KPIs are going to be different.

As I mentioned, we had found ourselves way out of the bell curve in terms of collection of A/R. I mentioned before our Average Days Sales of A/R was 120, whereas the best in our profession were 10 days, and the average in our industry was 60.

We got to work on the problem and, in a year and a half, we've gotten our average days down to 25 days, which resulted in literally hundreds of thousands of dollars in increased collections. We are no longer operating as a bank for our clients, loaning them interest-free money for four months. In fact, we expect our average to go into the negative as we switch to our monthly fixed fee model.

So, when figuring out what KPIs you should be monitoring, besides the ones that keep you up at night, be sure to look at the industry benchmarks. They know the metrics that matter. Looking at them will help you focus on the best benchmarks to monitor.

It can be really scary when you are trying to decide to make a change in your business. It was for us when we decided to spend more on marketing. But, having the dashboard allowed us to read the leading indicators and see that we were still flying steady. There is always a bit of trial and error when you are looking to get that edge, especially working to hire more people without slowing profit. It is a fine line when you are pushing the hyper-growth envelope.

When you are sailing, you are pushing your sails into the wind to get as tight an angle as possible. The high-end sailboats with the best equipment can be at 30% into the wind. If you push too far, you hit the dead zone and your sails start to flutter as the wind flows past them. If you don't push enough, you lose speed because the sails aren't catching as much wind as they can.

There are small pieces of fabric on the sails called tell tails that show you how well the sails are catching the wind. If they are standing out horizontally you are at maximum capacity, if they are down, or fluttering up, there is a problem. The telltales are your leading indicator, the speed of your boat is the lagging indicator.

The tell tails have been a standard indicator for as long as there have been sailboats; you don't have to figure that out on your own, every sail comes with tell tails attached. But, if you don't know how to read them, or that they are even there, then they don't do you much good. It's the same with any industry. The standards are there for you if you know where to look. They will help you get to maximum velocity in your business.

In accounting firms, as with most businesses, we can look at the best metrics for different sized companies. Accounting companies that average under $1 million in revenue generally have an increased profit margin because the owner is doing more of the actual hands-on work with the clients. As the company grows to between $1 to 5 million, there is a dip in the profit margin as the owner steps out of that role. Once an accounting firm reaches the $5 million range, the margins go back up.

The benchmarks are not meant to necessarily be your goals. We are higher on some, and that's fine as long as the additional money we are spending is producing increased cash. We look at the benchmarks from the industry and then analyze why ours are different. If it's increasing our profit, then I am comfortable with it.

Spending a few grand more on marketing is a simpler decision than increasing the staff. It's easy to turn off the marketing dollars if there is no change in the numbers. But hiring involves a commitment to people, their families and their livelihood. Because we needed to hire more people, we were banking on the growth continuing. It was a risk, but an educated one, not a gut decision. We knew what we needed to make payroll, what was in the pipeline, and how long it would take to collect on the work. We also had a consistent growth curve over a twelve-month cycle.

In addition, we know where to spend our money in order to increase profit. Spending money where you get the biggest bang takes a disciplined approach. Having a plan, a budget and closely watching our tell tails, helps keep us from making tempting, but foolish purchases. We are riding the wind instead of trying to sail right into it.

You should never spend higher than the industry average on categories that are not income-producing. Hiring more sales staff is investing in income production because they will increase your client base. Many times, purchasing equipment is investing in increased profit because the equipment allows you to work faster and more efficiently.

Sometimes, the investment can have short and long-term gains. We recently purchased six new computers for our team members. We have the short-term benefit of increased team members satisfaction with new computers, as well as the immediate depreciation we can take on the equipment. In addition, we have the longer-term gain of increased productivity and an increase in the bottom-line value of our company due to increasing profit (efficient work is profitable work).

One of the biggest advantages of owning a business, besides providing you a living, is the value of the business when it comes time to sell. Think about that! If you play your cards right, the business will not only give you a great living in the moment, it will keep on giving for many years to come! It can be an additional asset for retirement.

Every business owner should have an eye on his or her exit strategy. Having the books in order and systems and protocols in place allow for a smooth transition when it's time to parachute out. However, most owners have a grossly inflated value of their business.

This generally happens when businesses are not set up to run well without the original owner; an investor wants to buy the business, not you. If you don't have things set up in a way that a new person could easily step in and run things, then your company loses value when you leave. The dashboard, in most cases, is in the owner's head, not on paper. You might know how to run the company, but if there is no playbook to hand over to the next guy, you don't have anything worth buying.

A good CEO is one that plans a company that he can step away from. It should be running on auto-pilot, with the flight plan and the coordinates set. The CEO is like the pilot, having a cup of coffee while watching the dashboard for problems. They also are responsible to set new goals, but a new CEO wants to take control of a steady, well-greased machine—not something that will take a nosedive the moment you let go of the steering.

If you have your books in order and are best in class at the metrics that matter, you can demand a higher price point for your business than a similar competitor. The new owner will know what the profit margin is and how to keep things moving steadily through the transition. They will be inheriting employees that are highly satisfied and committed to their jobs.

There is a value to what is called the goodwill of a company, and it's included in the sale price of any business. This is an intangible asset that is included over and above the actual value of the business. It includes the value of the company's name in the community. This asset is not tangible but can be measured. It's the customer base, the employees, and the reputation of the company over the years. By having all the non-financial KPIs measured, as well as all the other numbers, it is possible to request top dollar for your goodwill.

So far, we've covered the importance of cash, keeping good and accurate books, how KPIs can drive your business and the value of measuring your company against the standards. But cash flow will always be the most important index you have for success. Let's dig a bit deeper to see how cash flow works.

MEASURING RESULTS

In what ways are you underperforming against the best in your industry?

_____

_____

_____

_____

If you don't know how you are doing against the rest of your industry, what is one action you will take to help improve that lack of knowledge?

_____

_____

_____

_____

"I will tell you the secret to getting rich on Wall Street. You try to be greedy when others are fearful. And you try to be fearful when others are greedy."

Warren Buffett

A Professional Accounting Corporation

Chapter Six

Where Did All My Cash Go?

Your accountant keeps telling you that you are making money, but where is it? You feel that, for all the increased revenue, you should be seeing more in the bank, and not knowing why your balance isn't higher is keeping you up at night. How can you keep on working harder and harder, with increased revenue, and still have the same amount in your bank account? How can you continue when there is not enough to invest back in the business?

These are the common questions we hear with new clients. They are stuck and seem unable to get to the next level. They feel like they are just running in place and never reaching the finish line. What the heck is going on?

Cash flow is the lifeblood of the business, but most business owners don't have the slightest idea how to track it. More often they are simply "managing by bank balance": they wake up in the morning and check the bank account to see if they can spend money that day. If there's money there, maybe they'll splurge for that piece of equipment they want. If there is no money in the bank, maybe they'll still splurge and just put it on a credit card.

When February or March rolls around, the business owner will gather all the bank statements together and start plugging them into their accounting system (or have their accountant do it). The accountant looks over the numbers and tells him he owes $30,000 in taxes, and he made $150,000 last year. But there is only $10,000 in the bank.

Sound familiar?

Developing the routines and habits necessary to allow you the impact of your decisions on your cash flow is the secret to sustainable business growth. Not only do these habits allow to grow sustainably, they also allow you to confidently pay yourself on a regular basis. The time-honored idea of paying yourself first is a good one. Too many owners are so focused on achieving maximal growth that they invest everything back into the business and forget about themselves. You have to ask yourself what you want and need to have a good lifestyle today. Fund your life now.

But how do you determine what you should pull out of the company to pay yourself?

It starts with looking at your own personal expenses and mapping out your monthly needs. Developing a personal budget allows you to get a handle on the business budget. Too often, business owners use their business account as a personal piggy bank, lending money out to themselves whenever they want, without planning ahead or considering the consequences to the company.

What do *you* need on a monthly basis? How much do you need for the mortgage, utilities, clothes on your back, and food on the table? Fund your needs first, including planning for the future with investments. Relying on the belief that you'll sell the business for 20X its worth is not a realistic retirement strategy. Your *needs* for funding your personal life are different from your *aspirations*. As the business grows, you can gradually include your ideal lifestyle in the budget and then assure that the business funds that.

I know my dad and I could scale down our personal incomes if for some reason the business started to slow down. But we enjoy our lifestyles, and since our business still has plenty of cash in the bank, we are happy to include that in the budget. There's no need to constantly pay the business first, or always re-invest all the profits. As long as you perform the proper cash flow planning routines in your business, you can pay yourself confidently and let your business actually provide you with a great life.

So, let's discuss those routines. At our CPA firm when it comes to our monthly planning sessions, we are not just looking back at how we did, but forward into the next month. We have a good idea what the revenue will look like because we have our clients set up on a monthly fee and can estimate new clients based on our historical conversions and planned marketing spend. We know what's going to be coming in, and then we look at our upcoming expenses. Can we cover payroll and other expenses? If not, what do we have in reserves to cover it?

Rather than thinking in terms of how much revenue you want to bring in, change your thinking to have this perspective: "How much cash do we want in the bank at any given moment to maintain a healthy business?" If we know we need $50,000 in the account for payroll on the 12th of the month, that makes all our spending decisions much clearer. Hoping the money will be there on the 12th isn't a good game plan.

If you are only focusing on increasing your revenue, you may miss those deadlines. Remember that growth sucks cash. The faster you are growing the faster you'll be spending cash, especially in a service industry. Let's say you have a tutoring company and are moving into a new region of your state. You'll need to hire new employees, but the revenue each employee produces is not going to be at maximum effectiveness right away.

First you have to recruit the employees, and maybe you need a new team leader to manage them. Then you have to train the new tutors and increase your advertising in that area to build up a client base. All of this takes time and money. The growth is great in the long run, but it's going to suck your cash. If you don't have a handle on cash flow, you may find yourself coming up short for a number of months, when you expected and counted on *instant* returns. How many months will it take?

Revenue does cover sins, but the devil is in the details. Growth needs to be manageable and predictable and that all comes back to cash flow. The only way you're going to know your cash flow is by starting with all the basics that we have discussed thus far. But you also have to know where your cash is going, and just as important is to know the timing of *when* that cash is going out. Planning your spending is easy to overlook, but it is a critical driver to health business growth.

All of this takes planning. A good look, once a month, at a rolling 12-month cash flow forecast, takes into account the ebbs and flows of the business. In the tutoring example, business will drop off dramatically in the summer months and holidays when families are on vacation. If your business is running a hotel, though, your busy season (and time of year with major cash inflows) would be exactly the opposite.

Growth tends to decrease the rate of cash flow as the business grows. Profit margins are always higher when a company is first starting out. That's because the owner is usually wearing many hats; front-desk, accounting, sales, and more. As the company grows, so does the infrastructure to support it. As it grows and becomes more complex, the profit margin tends to go down. There is a point, as the profit margin drops, where you'll wonder if growing is the right thing to do, but the key is whether you can shift from working in the business to managing it.

So many business owners hit the ceiling for growth at $300,000 - $500,000 in revenue and cannot manage the growth well enough to get any higher. They feel as if they made more money when they were smaller and decide to focus on maintaining the business instead of growing it.

It gets back to who you are as a business owner. If you are the artist who wanted to monetize their passion, then that may be a good decision. It takes a certain vision to shift to entrepreneur from artist and to step back to manage the growth rather than do the craft. And ultimately, you have to be ok with profit margins decreasing while you grow.

One of our clients was having the, "Where does the cash go?" blues when we first met him. His business was pulling in $15 million in revenue, yet he still stayed up at night worrying about money, simply because he didn't have a good understanding of his cash flow. When he was first starting his business, he would go shopping with his wife and find himself pulling things out of the shopping cart when her back was turned! This told us that, generally, his tolerance for risk was low.

We sat down with him and focused on his expenses; his revenue was not the problem, and he actually did have a couple million dollars in the bank. But, without the knowledge of his cash flow, his confidence in the business was low. We analyzed his cash flow monthly and looked at the numbers with him.

It turned out that he was personally spending much more than he realized. He had thirty to forty rental units that he was pouring a lot of cash into for renovations. In addition, his accounts receivables carried a balance, which meant his customers were essentially using him as a bank. Just getting a handle on his collections would significantly increase his cash flow. He also had racked up expenses on account in the previous months, and paid down the entire balance one month. The payment showed up, without being off-set by the expenses, in his income statement.

Even without increasing revenue, he was able to gain insight into his spending and cash flow and thus, his confidence in the business increased. We talked about tracking both of his businesses separately to see exactly where he was in relation to the real estate investments. In the meantime, his "Where did the money go?" concerns were answered. Things made sense to him, and he gained greater control of his cash flow. His wife could go shopping without her husband tagging along too!

This is a fairly common issue we encounter with new clients. It's not unusual for entrepreneurs to have a couple of different business ventures in the works. Unless they carefully track each one separately, it's difficult to see that, sometimes, one business is siphoning profits off another and may appear more successful than it actually is.

Even in a business that is well established and no longer worries about covering the monthly payroll, a clear understanding of cash in and out for those various ventures does wonders for the confidence level. No matter the size of a business, cash flow can keep you up at night.

In our business, we run these numbers for all of our CFO coaching clients. Definitely not enough people do this. They tend to lump their businesses' financials all together under one umbrella as "their business." They consider only the overall profit and not how each venture is affecting cash flow or whether it's worth dumping money into. Sometimes losing one aspect of a business is all that's needed to really increase profits. Without the numbers, and the cash, you may never know. Which brings us to the next topic: having a business model that speeds up, rather than slows down, your cash flow.

MEASURING RESULTS

How much revenue do you want? How much money in the bank?

_____

_____

_____

_____

How can you maintain growth with both?

_____

_____

_____

_____

"I love money. I love everything about it. I bought some pretty good stuff. Got me a $300 pair of socks. Got a fur sink. An electric dog polisher. A gasoline powered turtleneck sweater. And, of course, I bought some dumb stuff, too. "

Steve Martin

A Professional Accounting Corporation

Chapter Eight

Have a Business Model That Speeds up Cash as You Grow

Growth can drain your cash, but there are ways to keep money in your account as long as possible. The more cash-on-hand you have, the more patience you can have with your major business decisions. One change you can make pretty quickly is to look at getting some or all of your cash for a service up-front.

The Power of the Prepay

Certain businesses have been doing this for years; no one expects to get a hotel room and pay for it during the next billing cycle, but that is the norm for many service-based industries. In fact, that's the way many accounting firms run their billing. They will provide the service and then expect payment 30 to 45 days later. Lawyers often operate the same way. If they provide a service on the 3rd of November, they will review their billable time and send an invoice on the 8th of December, then finally collect (if all goes well) sometime in mid-January.

Amazon ran at a loss for years but was able to continue to grow rapidly because their business model was set up to generate cash up front. The idea was to accelerate the revenue stream regardless of profitability and take advantage of the power of that cash.

Uber used this technique quite successfully when they changed their billing approach. At first, they used to give an estimate of the cost, say between $15 and $18, and then collect after the ride had been provided. When they shifted to a set fee, along with "surge rates" during busy times, the costs actually increased for most rides. At the same time, customer satisfaction also increased. Customers preferred knowing exactly what they would be paying, even if it was a bit higher.

In addition, although it may not seem like the cash was in hand that much sooner, if you multiply the 20 or 30 minutes longer that Uber had that cash by the hundreds of thousands of transactions that were happening all around the world, it was substantial.

When a business is first starting out, it's harder to demand the cash up-front. Every customer seems essential and you want to please them, and there is pressure to let them treat you like their bank. But don't do it. Set your policies early on so you never allow it to become a major issue. Training existing clients to change their ways is much more difficult than setting ground rules for new clients.

We are starting to see a movement in certain medical professions where the offices are getting away from billing insurance companies all together and, instead, offering concierge services for private pay. Their clients pay a yearly fee to be a private customer, along with a monthly payment. In return, they get premium treatment that is no longer dictated by the insurance companies. The medical offices are seeing fewer patients but getting much more revenue per client. The clients are getting personalized attention without getting rushed out the door.

We started doing basically the same thing in our business. We have an initial service fee and then monthly payments. Essentially, our clients are paying for their tax return when they pay us the yearly fee in January. We may have lost a few clients when we changed our procedures, but those that came on board are highly committed to our company and love the customized attention they receive. When they need to pick up the phone and ask a quick question, they aren't worried about getting charged for our time. We are at their service, and that piece of mind is worth the added expense.

How and when you collect can mean the difference between success and failure in any sized business. Always look for opportunities to collect up front and you'll start to feel the power that cash in the bank has for your business. The worries of meeting your expenses start to dissipate as your collections are more evenly spread across the month and year.

This technique also allows you to clearly estimate your future collections and know when and how much money will be in the bank. You'll no longer be dependent on someone in your office getting the bill in the mail, and the client then eventually responding to that bill. You'll see your AR start to fall dramatically and your average cash reserve climb, along with your confidence.

It goes back to being able to be proactive rather than reactive. There will no longer be a billing frenzy when you realize you will be short for payroll and you have to drop everything in an effort to call clients and beg for payment.

With the cash in your account, instead of your AR column, your purchasing power goes up, as well as your ability to expand comfortably. That money can be put to use, generating additional income, by investing in the business, instead of floating out there somewhere in the black hole. Each day that payment is delayed is a loss of return on your possible investment.

Check with Vendors

Another way to increase your cash flow is to look at the other side of the equation, in your Accounts Payable. Hopefully, you have developed good relationships with your vendors as you've grown. They are usually motivated to keep your business and will often be willing to give you more favorable terms if you ask for them. This is especially true if you are a large buyer for them. The more leverage you have, the better terms you will be able to negotiate.

Try to get at least a net 30 or net 60 term—meaning you pay 30 or 60 days after you receive their bill. Don't worry about the small vendors, focus on your larger ones. Always try to avoid upfront payments and don't pay a bill until it's due. The longer that money is in your hands, the more it works for you (Unless you're paying your accountant. Then always pay them on time).

Sometimes there is an advantage to putting certain payments on a credit card or some other line of credit. This only works if you have a good handle on your debt and are generally able to pay the line of credit off each month. Basically, you are getting your 30-day float and pushing that payment into the following month. If, at the same time, you are collecting your own revenue up front, then your cash in the bank is increased and the payroll or other major expense due mid-month is no problem.

Review Your "Free" Services

Another way to improve your cash is to re-assess any services that you may be giving away for free as a promotion. We used to give a free phone consultation to potential new clients, and we gave away all of our unique strategies and valuable information on that first call. The trouble with our approach was that we were giving them tons of valuable information at no charge. It got to the point that my dad and I were too busy to make these calls, so we developed a sales staff to manage them.

Now we were paying for the sales team, the infrastructure, and all the associated management costs. It was becoming quite an expensive process for us, so we decided to tweak things a bit. Now, we give them the free half-hour consultation call, but we have structured our question-asking process so that we uncover everything they are leaving on the table and their estimated potential savings.

If they want answers, we offer them a 30-40 page comprehensive tax report that lays it all out, and they paid us for that report and access to the strategies (paid up front, of course). This new process, not only covers the costs for our team of consultants, it also increases cash flow. As an added benefit, more clients sign on to our yearly program than did with the prior "free" call. Once the clients see our tax plan and how much money we can save them each year, they want the full package.

If you decide to change to a prepayment model, be sure you also take a look at your workflow management system to be sure you can handle the increased capacity and don't get bottle-necked with the work. You will have to review your scheduling process as well. Smoothing out cash flow throughout the month and knowing when you will be paid and how much work you have will transform your business.

I've always admired the business savvy of The Disney Company; they are experts in how they implement many of the processes we are discussing. If you haven't already been, I'd recommend a trip, it's great fun and you'll also see some great business lessons in action.

For example, they use these wonderful little gadgets called Magic Bands for clients that control your entire experience during your stay—the "keys to the kingdom," if you will. You swipe them to get in the park, to buy food, and even souvenirs at the gift shop. They will send you a plain old gray magic band for free, but, for only $29.95, you can have a Mickey Mouse magic band! Who isn't going to go for that! And it's paid for before your trip begins, of course.

What are the areas in your business where you are giving away something of *value* to your clients for free? The key here is that it should be something the client actually values. We aren't going to charge extra for printing our a second paper copy of their tax return—that's called nickel-and-diming—but they are excited to pay for our tax plan report because it has immense value.

Another example would be someone selling real estate: rather than charging an "administration fee" for all the paperwork, why not charge a "staging fee" to decorate their house during the listing instead? People are way more excited to pay for their house looking pretty than they are for a paperwork charge. What services are your clients excited about in your business?

Speeding up your cash flow is the secret to any successful business. Whether you are a small, one-person operation or a $25 million company, this holds true. Even a hairdresser can try selling a package of 10 prepaid haircuts for a small discount, or offer the deluxe package that includes a shoulder massage and a bottle of special product. Offering clients a variety of options gives them more control, and they rarely pick the bare-bones option.

How you structure payments for your services can always be tweaked to increase cash flow. Having more cash on hand gives you the power to make the changes you are dreaming about. It allows you to be in charge, calling the shots, instead of always feeling as if you are behind the eight-ball with no clear shots in sight. You can run the table instead of having to go for the double-bank impossible long shot just to stay in the game.

As your collections become smoother and more predictable, it will be that much easier to develop a reasonable budget. You will be able to cover your monthly bills more easily, maintain your current lifestyle and save for retirement. It also allows you to build up the cash reserves needed for the inevitable ebbs and flows of your business, as well as the next economic downturn.

MEASURING RESULTS

How do you currently go about getting your money, your income, payment for your services, etc.?

_____

_____

_____

_____

How can you improve your system?

_____

_____

_____

_____

"What we really want to do is what we are really meant to do. When we do what we are meant to do, money comes to us, doors open for us, we feel useful, and the work we do feels like play to us."

Julia Cameron

A Professional Accounting Corporation

Chapter Nine

Cash Reserves to Weather the Economic Downturns

Having cash reserves has never been more important than in the recent economic crisis created by the COVID-19 pandemic. Many businesses learned that lesson the hard way. If you are doing everything we've talked about in the prior chapters, then you'll have no trouble stashing away a reserve for tough times.

The general consensus is to have somewhere between 2-6 months of expenses in the bank at all times that is readily available. By expenses, we mean your costs of doing business each month, not your monthly revenue. So, if the cash out each month to cover your overhead (and your own minimum personal expenses needed from the business) is $10,000, you'll want between $20,000 to $60,000 available.

The determination as to the exact amount depends on how predictable your revenue is. This is the reason that subscription model businesses are twice as valuable as other businesses. Their revenue is very predictable. They might lose a client here or there, but can generally count on a steady stream of cash.

If your business is more volatile, you'll need more in reserve. If you are in the real estate business, for example, things can go dry for months on end, as we saw in 2008— where no one could sell a house because so many were underwater. Tons of real estate agents closed their doors and scrambled for any kind of work they could find.

They are notorious, in a hot market, for living high on the hog and not saving. It always seems like real estate is going to go up and up. The trouble is that it is never in a straight line! The lull happens and many real estate agents get knocked out of the game.

Once you get into a negative balance on your cash, the odds are stacked against you incredibly high. It is almost impossible to climb out of that hole. This is especially true for low-margin businesses like restaurants; most of them operate on such a razor thin margin that the additional loan repayment for going negative is too much for them to carry.

That's why so many restaurants crashed and burned with COVID-19. Even the extremely successful ones, in terms of customers coming through the door, apparently didn't have enough cash reserves to weather the storm of being shut down. When things get tough is when you see who has planned best. The greatest transfer of wealth occurs during recessions. It's said that the ones that have a seven-figure account grow it to eight, and the ones with an eight-figure account grow to nine. The ones with inadequate reserves lose everything.

During the good times, it's important to have the discipline to save for the bad times. If you are having some trouble saving up reserves, even during the good times, you might want to consider getting a line of credit. The banks are more likely to give out loans when the economy is cranking along. That all dries up during economic crises—which happens to also be when businesses need it the most. If you get that line of credit in the good times, you have the opportunity to draw against it on a rainy day.

So where do you put this stash of reserves? It's best to put it somewhere that is hard to get to, maybe a treasury bill, money market, or a separate bank account that's not connected to your operating account. One of my clients put it in a bank that was a forty-minute drive away, and he didn't get a debit card or checking account with it. Put up some kind of barrier to prevent easy access so you can forget that the money is there. One place not to put it is on black at the casino!

COVID-19 has been a unique experience. We helped hundreds of clients get PPP loans. Without those, many clients would have gone down. In California we've had a total shutdown at the beginning with partial openings, and who knows where we are heading in 2021? It's more important than ever to get your reserves ready. One thing we've learned through this is that we do not want to count on the government to bail us out.

According to Business Insider, most small businesses have an average cash reserve of just enough to stay open for 27 days. Labor intensive businesses have even less, with restaurants averaging just 16 days of reserves. Very few had over 45 days, and over 25% have less than 13 days of reserve cash. That means if all money stopped coming through the door, they would be able to stay open for less than 2 weeks!

A business owner will look at his or her account and think that $10,000 is a great buffer, but that's not going to keep you in business. The businesses we all thought were killing it seemed to be some of the first to fail. As Warren Buffet observed:

"Only when the tide goes out do you discover who's been swimming naked."

For businesses that are prepared for the downturns, tough times can be a boom since so many of their competitors go out of business. In my firm, we increased our marketing and hired a new recruiter to gather up some great talent that was laid off from other businesses. Our sales have been growing faster than ever.

So, these cash reserves can be used in the downturn for defense - to save your business from failure, but also for offense - to take advantage of the closure of so many businesses. You can take the reserves during the downturns and use them for growth. Someone has to be there to pick up the pieces, it might as well be you. Get ready for the bad times and you will be positioned to thrive.

The companies that have thrived during the pandemic are the ones that were able to do the pivot, and had the means to go in a new direction. It's not luck, it's all about being positioned to make a pivot when needed. Having your KPIs in place allows you to see the writing on the wall before most of your competition will, and then having the reserves makes the pivot possible.

Having the infrastructure and technology to quickly shift processes is what made the transition to online services smoother, and kept many businesses afloat. They didn't have a crystal ball telling them this pandemic was coming. What they did have in common is a solid cash flow plan and a reserve that allowed them to afford the resources to make a shift happen.

In addition, I suspect that there was clarity of purpose. If you know your business, its strengths and how it is capable of helping people, then it's easier to innovate. In other words, if you know your "why" the other questions can find a way. If your purpose is to help your clients live a better life, you will find a way to be of service to them. Once you can think about your clients' needs, and not just worry about your own survival, then you will find a path forward. This is difficult if you are not on strong financial footing.

We had the confidence to know our company was going to be able to ride out this current situation, and that allowed us to focus on our clients' needs. We jumped in, innovated and offered our clients what they needed most; we worked with them to obtain loans, helped with ideas to invest in revenue-producing activities, and talked strategies to free up cash.

Yes, these are tough times for any business, but it is possible to thrive in a downturn. If you are getting slammed now, don't give up. It's never too late to start taking the necessary steps towards a more secure future. The challenges provide a test-by-fire to show you where your weaknesses are. It's time to take those lessons and double down on yourself and your business.

MEASURING RESULTS

What does your cash reserve currently look like?

_____

_____

_____

_____

What do you want it to look like and by what date can you commit to reaching that target?

_____

_____

_____

_____

"A nickel ain't worth a dime anymore."

Yogi Berra

A Professional Accounting Corporation

Chapter Ten

Utilize Your CPA for Tax Planning to Lower Your Largest Expense - Taxes

No one seems to think about taxes as the largest expense of your life, but it often is! It's as if you had to pay all of your payroll in one check and never gave it a thought until a few months before it was due. That would be crazy, yet many business owners treat taxes that way.

Right now, we are in a historically low tax time. In the 50s, the top tax bracket was 94%. I believe that taxes are only going up from here. If you are having difficulty paying your taxes, you should start considering ways to get a handle on them now.

Most people meet their accountants once a year, around February or March, to "do their taxes." By then, it's too late to have any significant effect and the accountant is merely a historian, assisting with the documentation and filing of the forms. This is the way most accountants do business. They make all their money during "tax season."

Actually, this is the worst possible time for you to begin looking at your taxes. It's too late to make a difference to the actual expenses, assets or revenue for the year. There are many things that you can do throughout the year to minimize your tax burden, but that would mean being proactive about them. Also, most tax accountants are at their most stressed and overworked in those months running up to April 15th and may not do their best work for you.

An accountant is not a magician; the work to lower your tax burden and increase your profits is ongoing, it's not juggling the numbers and waving a magic wand to make taxes go away. A good accountant is a coach and an educator, teaching you how to run your business properly to achieve success. I think you understand by now that "success" means cash in the bank.

At the very least, you should meet in early December, when it's still possible to make some last-minute changes to your income. In December, we can still give you an action plan to help mitigate the taxes, and run the numbers to project your annual income so you know what you will most likely owe on April 15th. This gives you five more months to get your finances in order for what is coming. Our clients usually make a profit by hiring us for a tax review, and we almost always save a company thousands more than they pay us!

The more common scenario is a business owner meeting their accountant after the year is over. They hand over their package of information and sit by the phone, waiting for the news, having no idea what they owe. By then, there is not much an accountant can do for you to change the tax number except help you put some money in a retirement fund to shield it. Putting money into an IRA is great, but it is just barely scratching the surface on what you can do to lower your taxes. There is so much more to be done.

Once that ball drops at midnight in Times Square and Ryan Seacrest wishes the world a Happy New Year, it's game over. There is nothing to be done to change those numbers. Hopefully, you've put some money aside for taxes and it's somewhere in the general ballpark of what you are going to owe. The only good news is that you can start to make changes for the year to come so you are prepared for the next April 15th.

Depending on how rapidly your business is growing, you should meet more often, not just at year-end. For businesses that are at or over 20% growth, I suggest at least quarterly meetings.

For example, we work with a company that sells clothes online. December is generally the best month of the year for them, so it's hard to project the bottom line in revenue. But we've already taken that into account and made contingency plans for them.

They know that, if they make a certain amount in December, then they should cut these checks before the end of the year. If they make another amount, then they have different action items. We don't even have to meet them, they just call and tell us the amount, and we confirm the plan.

Another rule of thumb to live by as a business owner: If your CPA is not a profit center for you, then you have the wrong CPA.

If your business is mostly steady from year to year, you don't have to meet as often. You can follow the plan and just check in to see if the tax code has changed. But, if you are growing 20 or 30%, you are growing in dog years—the business in June is a different animal than it was in January. There are completely different tax strategies for a company that has more employees or more revenue than another.

In the US, there are basically two separate tax codes, one for employees and one for business owners. With employees, they may be able to deduct some of their mortgage, charitable donations, property and state taxes. But there is a limit to what we can do for them. Most business owners still operate under this system, but there is a whole world of possibilities in the tax code for them that they may not even be aware of.

The business tax codes are so complicated and thick that if you printed them all out and had them in a room between us, a bullet from your Magnum45 would not be able to pierce the tax code to reach me. There is a wealth of information in there that can save you money on your taxes.

On top of the two different tax codes, there are essentially two types of tax planning for business owners: tax planning for *permanent* savings and planning for *deferring* taxes. By permanent savings, we mean that you get your deduction and never have to pay it back. It's a one-time, yearly, permanent tax deduction. Those are the tax savings you go after first.

For example, by forming an S corp, you can minimize the dreaded self-employment tax that burdens so many small businesses. It's possible to save as much as $13,000 a year in taxes this way. This tax savings is permanent and is available each year, meaning you never have to pay those self-employment taxes back at any time in the future.

Another strategy that provides a permanent savings is to hire your children. There are tax savings that can be realized for hiring your children who are under 18 years of age, and even ways to have your adult children establish a support company to yours and then hire their children, your grandchildren.

There are also strategies that allow for tax savings when hiring your adult children, but, as with hiring children under the age of 18, there are a lot of variables that need to be discussed with your CPA. For the purposes of this book, you should investigate the permanent tax savings that are available to you if this strategy is properly executed.

Deferral strategies, on the other hand, mean you get the deduction now but will eventually pay the tax back. There are several ways available to defer taxes. For example, by putting the maximum amount in your 401K, you are deferring tax on that income until you withdraw it during your retirement. It is still likely a good strategy since you can keep the tax savings as cash in your business and use the money to generate even more cash, but that analysis must be made to see if the opportunity is worth the savings.

Another great strategy for tax savings is to prepay some of your next year's expenses in December. You would need to be on a cash basis with your accounting, not accrual. Again, the idea behind this strategy is to keep the taxes in your hands as long as possible, where you can use it to generate income. You'll have to pay the taxes on the income the following year, but you'll also have the opportunity to defer further taxes by prepaying additional expenses that year as well.

This allows you to keep more money in the business where it can be used in a revenue-generating capacity. Think of these tax deferments as an interest-free loan from the government. If you invest that cash and it generates a 20 or 30% return to the business's bottom line, you've made a profit on money that otherwise would have gone to taxes. When you eventually pay them, you have essentially lowered your tax expense.

One of our clients is a construction company that had their best year a couple years ago. Their profit was 2.2 million, and they had 1.1 million in the bank. But 1 million of that was set to go for taxes. We implemented various tax strategies and the tax bill ended up being $250k instead. Hiring our company saved them $750,000, but we have saved other companies millions in taxes, year after year. We educated another client of ours, who has four children, on how to get the kids on the payroll. The savings from that strategy, combined with using the Augusta rule (an IRS rule which allows you to rent your house out for 14 days a year tax-free), they were able to take an additional $62,000 tax deduction.

If you take one of these "tax loans" from the government and "flex it on the 'gram" by buying a

Lamborghini, you have defeated the purpose! Instead, put it into whatever is limiting your capacity for growth. That may be increasing your employee headcount, or investing in equipment or marketing, for example.

There has been a lot of chatter this year about wealthy people avoiding taxes. But every business owner I know spends this savings to hire people and create growth. It's a win-win for their new employees and the economy in general. Tax deferment is one of the most powerful tools we have to increase a business's cash flow and generate growth. If you do not gleefully look forward to a meeting with your CPA, then there is something wrong!

MEASURING RESULTS

How often do you currently do tax planning for your business or personal taxes?

_____

_____

_____

_____

What is one activity or strategy you can implement to lower your tax bill starting today?

_____

_____

_____

_____

"Many people take no care of their money till they come nearly to the end of it, and others do just the same with their time."

Johann Wolfgang von Goethe

A Professional Accounting Corporation

Chapter Eleven

Review Your Financial Terms - Both Length of Loans and Interest Rates

Having debt is almost always part of starting and growing a business. But, if you are not careful, paying interest can be a clever nickname for "throwing your money in the garbage." It's critical to look for ways to reduce the expense of your debt, whether it's personal or business. During good times, it's easier to negotiate with banks and credit card companies to get a lower rate on debt. When you're paying a high-interest rate on debt, it's like a financial cancer inside your business, eating away at your cash.

Think of it this way. We all appreciate the dramatic difference of a 10% rate of return on our investments versus a

2% return. We'll spend hours trying to figure out a way to squeeze even 1% more of interest on our savings. We'll carefully review our interest-bearing accounts and investments each month and make adjustments to improve our returns.

Yet, when we *pay* interest on debt, we do not give it the same scrutiny—even though it's the same concept, just in reverse. You are losing more money each month with every percent of interest on debt. Any action you can take, large or small, to reduce the interest on your debt is putting money in your hands instead of the banks'.

Many people in a bind will try switching debt to a six-month, interest-free credit card, but I find these deals to be super dangerous and I don't recommend them. But you can negotiate. Can I change from 18% to 15%, or lengthen a loan from 3 years to 5 years? These tactics put the cash in your hands longer where you can use it for growth. Whenever you are deciding whether or not to take on debt, it's important to consider the return on the investment you are making with the cash from that debt. If you are able to get a cash injection through a loan at a 3 or 4% rate of interest, and put that into a business that has a proven, steady growth of 18 to 20%, then that is a good use of debt.

But, if you are struggling with your growth, then debt can easily become the anchor that finally sinks you. Rather than grabbing for more debt, start first by considering the other strategies we've talked about to increase cash flow. Also work to reduce the interest and work at paying the debt down as quickly as possible.

Many business owners start their ventures on the backs of credit cards, and sometimes it's a necessity. If you are burdened with a lot of personal debt, either from starting your business, funding your education or even from a medical emergency, there is a way to shift that debt from personal to business, as long as your business is generating a decent return.

What I recommend in these cases, is for my client to obtain a business credit card, and begin to use it to pay for regular business expenses. Then, instead of paying off that business card, take the cash that would have been used to pay your business expenses as a profit distribution, and use it to pay off the personal credit cards faster. You may think that is just transferring debt from one card to the next, except for one important difference - business interest is a tax deduction while personal interest isn't. This small adjustment can save you thousands every year, and effectively cut your interest rate by one third simply from making the interest tax deductible.

Another way of shifting personal expenses to the business is to plan your trips to include a legitimate business function. Going to a conference in an exotic location is a perfect example. Then, much of the expense of the vacation, your travel, hotel and dining, can be deducted as a business expense. Check with your CPA (or reach out to my firm) for specific guidance on how to make sure your trips can be legitimately deducted as expenses in your business.

There are many more techniques for improving your capacity to reduce your debt. The use of a proactive CPA, instead of a bean-counting accountant, can literally save you thousands of dollars each year. It can be the difference between prosperity and bankruptcy.

Another way to negotiate with the banks for a lower interest rate is to consider getting your books audited. Most people run when they hear the word audit, but in this case, it can potentially save you thousands of dollars.

Audits are performed by an independent CPA who certifies your books are solid and accurate. Banks are much more likely to give you favorable rates if your books have been audited. The most companies we see that benefit the most from this are ones that have a lot of equipment, like a construction company, or are carrying a lot of debt. In some cases, taking that loan to pay down other loans with higher interest rates can be an effective way of increasing cash flow.

We started to work with a client that had $3 million in loans on the books with a 10% interest rate. They never thought to get an audit, which they only associated with the IRS. We recommended an audit, and subsequently, their interest rate went from 10% to 6%, saving them a whopping $120,000 a year. The audit was a one-time $40,000 expense, but the return on investment was phenomenal and continued yearly.

Another situation where an audit is helpful is when you are considering selling all or part of your business. Companies whose books have been audited consistently for several years running nearly always command a higher multiple than businesses who have been had an audit.

Never underestimate the power of a great CPA!

MEASURING RESULTS

What does your debt look like? Amount and length?

_____

_____

_____

_____

What's the best course of action to take over it? What's the best plan of attack?

_____

_____

_____

_____

"Formal education will make you a living; self-education will make you a fortune."

Jim Rohn

A Professional Accounting Corporation

Chapter Twelve

Culture Drives Profitability

Having a company culture is not about the foosball table in the break room, and it's not just for the big millennial companies like Google, Square or Twitter. Every company has a culture, whether you know it or not and, if you don't take the time to be intentional with the culture, one will develop without your input.

Culture is one of those things that is hard to define, but you know it when you see it. It's found in the attitude that your employees project towards the company, the way a company communicates with its employees and clients, and even in the layout of the offices. If the owner values transparency, open communication and innovation, there will be a culture that supports employee suggestions and ideas. Culture in a business-setting transcends politics, religion, race and all the other things that can separate people in society. If you develop a clear company culture, people from all sorts of different walks of life can come together and work as a team for the betterment of the business.

Of course, a person that is a vegan is unlikely to seek employment at a meat packing company, so there is a good deal of self-selection that occurs. That's part of the reason that the company culture should be obvious to the public as well. They say good marketing attracts the clients you want and repels the clients you don't; good culture does that but for your team members.

You are only as good as your team. How your employees see the business will inform how they do their job. That message has to be consistent and come from the top. It's like a crew team rowing in the same direction compared to one out of sync. The coxswain can see the finish line and the team relies on his or her guidance to get them there. You not only cross the finish line faster, your profits are also tied to the quality of your team's work. But, as a company grows, it's easy for different departments to become more isolated from each other and focus on their own individualized goals, which can even be opposed to each other's.

119

You may have a sales team that is laser focused on bringing as many new clients in the door as possible, while the team responsible for delivering your service is looking to reduce total turnaround time. This is when it becomes absolutely critical to have teamwide goals that push and pull against each department in opposing ways.

Once your departments become at odds with each other and have conflicting and contradictory goals, and more importantly value their individual department goals over the entire organization's goals, your company begins to drift— being pushed in one direction after the other, but making no progress in the right direction. This is the demise of many companies as they experience growth and then hit a plateau and become more and more disorganized and frayed.

It's imperative to set company-wide goals and actively work to have a tight team across all departments. This is not about some feel-good, warm and fuzzy pride in the company name - well not only about that. But, it's about the survival of your company and the bottom line. It's as important as providing basic equipment and office space for everyone to do their work.

At my firm we set goals, and associated performance metrics, each quarter for the company. The goals are usually just one or two critical metrics that are opposed to each other so that the departments are forced to look outside of their narrow view to see performance as a whole. We may set the number of tax plans as one metric, but also include tax return turnaround time as another. Now, instead of the sales and accounting departments working independently from each other, they have to put their collective heads together to reach the goals.

Along with goals, you also have to incentivize your staff and make it worth their trouble for helping the company grow, each quarter and each year. We set our targets and then celebrate each goal reached. One year we rewarded our employees with seats behind home base at a San Francisco Giants game, another year, we had go-cart races. This turns somewhat mundane numbers, such as the number of tax plans completed, into the talk at the water fountain.

Each quarter has its own theme associated with it. This quarter, we Disneyfied, with the theme being "A Whole New World." By changing the themes and goals quarterly, it keeps everyone focused and things fresh. No one can sprint for an entire year (although 2020 certainly felt like a full year sprint), but most of us can focus on a three-month goal, especially if there are concrete rewards. We try to make the rewards experiences that most employees wouldn't experience otherwise. Some of our top employees may be able to afford those seats in the 2nd row behind home-base, but most

121

wouldn't splurge on something like that. It has to be special and memorable for all!

Once we took the team hot air ballooning over Napa Valley, our theme that quarter was "Following Up." This quarter, the theme is "Seal Team Thirty-Six," because we want to get to thirty-six employees. Seal teams do a lot of cross-training with different skills. We want everyone to understand all the different aspects of the company. One of the potential awards will be to take the team paintballing. Our goals are in levels, there is super-green, green, yellow or red, depending on how well the goal is reached. There are rewards for each.

We have gotten so good at incentivizing our team, that we now do consulting with our larger Virtual CFO clients on how to maintain focus and excitement in their business and develop a positive culture. They are willing to pay for this service because they understand, first-hand, the financial benefit of a motivated, synchronized team.

We started with a team of four, and it took some time to work things out. Even with just four of us, there are still 24 possible lines of communication. When we missed out on setting a goal for a quarter, we noticed we didn't do as well. Now, we start to discuss the future themes and goals a few weeks before the end of the quarter. There is nothing like having a company-wide goal to really get everyone focused

122

and working together. Sometimes we would set a massive goal that was quite a challenge to reach. Our employees have always pushed at the end to cross the finish line. It does wonders for our shared confidence when we achieve a major come-from-behind goal at the super green level.

As an organization, we need collective habits and structures to follow, that's part of developing a positive business culture. We hone our processes each time we reach a difficult goal together. As we continue this practice of setting goals as a cohesive group, we've also developed and sharpened our skills. At first, there was not the full, all-in, level of commitment that we see now. We've grown together as a company, just the way a family, working together to overcome hardship, grows from the experience.

When beginning this process, don't try to be something you are not. If you want to rule the company with an iron fist and not involve employees in the decision-making process, then you will attract and retain employees that want that type of environment. For us, teamwork is our first priority and top-ranked core value, so our employees operate with that mindset. I believe that is why we have been selected as one of the top twenty firms to work for in the US by Accounting Today.

Listen to Your Clients and Employees

If you have a consistent, clear message and culture, the clients and employees who sign on with you are more likely to stay, and that translates into profits. Once you get them both on board, keeping them should be one of your key, measurable goals.

Keeping a client is MUCH less expensive than going out and getting a new one. It's exciting to chase a client and put together a marketing plan, but the day-to-day of client service is where you find the gold. The actual cost of a new client is not just the marketing dollars, it's the TIME involved with getting to know them and developing the relationship. The cost of the infrastructure for finding them and then learning what they want is also a factor. It's the total of all the time, energy and resources involved, from the initial on-boarding, to the paperwork and more.

The same goes for keeping your employees. Employee turn-over should be one of the KPIs that is regularly monitored. The costs of a new employee go far beyond the recruiting costs. There is also the learning curve involved and the time that one of our better employees has to put aside to train. It can slow your trajectory as you plug the new employee into the system. The fewer disruptions in your staff the better.

We have a process for asking questions of our clients and employees that goes beyond the NPS (Net Promoter Score, see page 50) which we send out several times a year. We also have, embedded in our processes, the time to ask questions of our clients and employees, and also to listen to the answers.

We regularly send out anonymous questionnaires, using Typeform or SurveyMonkey, to get employee feedback. In these anonymous surveys we do give the employee the opportunity to share their name, as most employees enjoy being recognized for their ideas and contributions. The questions are these: "What should we be doing that we are not? What should we stop doing? What should we start doing?"

Once you ask the questions, you have to close the loop and respond to them. Even if you are not going to use the idea, discuss the reasons why, maybe the timing just isn't right even if it's a good idea. We look at all the answers at our quarterly meeting and review them with our leadership team.

One employee, who was involved in onboarding, let us know that, when they ask a new client for a particular piece of information, often the client responded with, "I've already sent that form in, why are you asking for it again?" Onboarding is the first client experience with our company and can set the tone for the future relationship. Our employee suggested a

New Client Intake Form to prevent this from occurring. It was a simple, yet powerful addition to our new client onboarding process that we had missed.

We also send emails asking for feedback from our clients, "How was your experience with our company?" "What else are you looking for?" "What would make us a 10?" Then, we categorize the client comments and review them at our semi-annual meeting. If we had six complaints about our response time, and four about our prices, we can decide if and how to act on those. Sometimes, the loudest complaints come from a client who doesn't fit in within our ideal client criteria, and that certainly impacts whether we decide to make significant system changes.

Our goal is to design systems that delight and wow our *ideal* client—not just anyone who walks through our doors. It's always the case that 90% of the problems come from 10% of the clients, and we are absolutely not afraid to disengage from the wrong clients. But, if the complaints come from clients that you respect and want to retain, then it's time to act.

Communication goes two ways. We try to keep the lines of communication open with our clients and employees, but we also need to put our message out there to the larger community, and this is where social media comes in. If you are not using social media to create growth and project your business culture, you are not just rowing in the wrong direction, you're dead in the water!

MEASURING RESULTS

What does the culture of your company currently look like?

_____

_____

_____

_____

How do you want it to look?

_____

_____

_____

_____

"Empty pockets never held anyone back. Only empty heads and empty hearts can do that."

Norman Vincent Peale

A Professional Accounting Corporation

Bonus Chapter

Social Media Strategies to Grow Your Business

We have built a strong business through social media and many people have asked me to share about this. Marketing is not complete without social media being front and center.

But, before you jump in on trying to acquire a barrage of new customers, first focus on the basics of increasing cash flow, growing your business and creating a company culture. Then, when it's time to turn on the gas, start building your social media accounts and focus on really scaling.

Contrary to what many believe, this is a time-consuming process that is not easy or free.

I've developed what I call the three Cs of social media strategy: Content, Community and Conversion. The content will drive your popularity, if you offer something of value.

Content

I always say that, as someone who primarily shares about taxes and numbers (yawn), if I can build an audience and business through social media then nobody else has an excuse! I'm currently at 120,000 followers and climbing. How does this happen to an accountant? By being the expert they can turn to with their questions and having relevant content. I am teaching and sharing my knowledge. What do you have to teach others about your business?

In many ways, the content is the easy part. I started by answering the questions I hear my new clients ask me every day. Every business owner is asked the same 10 questions, over and over again. They may change over time depending on the economic climate. But, if they are relevant questions, you'll hear them more than once. I always write down questions I am asked and, if it seems like it would help other business owners, I'll write out the answers and convert that into a video or written post.

Once you develop a good following, then your audience will help you find additional content, all you have to do is ask them what they want to know. Lately, I've written about:

The Number One Thing to Lower Your Tax Bill
How to Make Every Day Black Friday
The Importance of Meeting Rhythms in Your Business
Gratitude (for Thanksgiving)

I am providing (in my humble opinion) insanely valuable content, sharing my personal values and teaching people how to lower their taxes and increase cash-flow in my Instagram posts. By doing so, I am intentionally creating Community.

Community

When I go to events, I have recently experienced the strange phenomenon of random attendees wanting to take a picture with me. It was a super bizarre feeling the first time it happened, but I learned that when people see you through the lens of a camera it automatically confers on you this quasi-celebrity status. Why does this happen? Because my followers feel that they know me. I have given them information they can use the next day to improve their businesses, and they appreciate my efforts. I share about my family and kids and I talk about my values. They are my tribe.

Russel Brunson, founder of ClickFunnels, gave me the idea to give a name to the community; for me, it's "Tax Savers." So, I start each video with, "What's Up Tax Savers?" Now my followers have an identity, and they are proud to be a Tax Saver with me.

Intuit, a Fortune 100 company, recently hired me to do a video promotion for their QuickBooks Payroll product, and in the videos, they wanted me to say, "What's up Tax Savers?" They see the strength of our tribe and want to be considered a part of it. By creating a Community, you are providing people an opportunity to feel like a part of something. It's really cool when there is interaction between members and not just with me.

Conversion

Of course, the ultimate goal of any social media program is to convert "followers" to clients.

We want to get in personal contact with potential clients that meet us on social media. Once I can get someone on the phone and tell them that I can save them $40k in taxes, they want to come on board.

The first step is to capture an email or phone number. I do this by offering a free consultation. Sometimes a follower will shoot me a message with questions and this gives me the chance to offer to hop on the phone with them. I am never directly asking followers to be clients, but I am using every opportunity to show them the benefits.

Stick with it! It takes time and money to build a following. When I first approached my dad with the idea, he thought I was crazy! But I was determined. I'd always loved marketing and that differentiates me from most CPAs. I knew the cost can be prohibitive, especially upfront when you are just getting started and not seeing an immediate return. But it pays amazing dividends.

Once you go all in, you need to be consistent with your posts, whether you post daily or weekly, don't miss a post. Then, be patient. Once you hit around 10,000 followers, in my experience, things can really take off. It's how I became connected with some very high-level companies and influential people in the entrepreneur space. And people who have been following me for a while are literally rooting for my journey. As such, I not only teach, I motivate. And that is something I didn't see coming, at first. But now, I've embraced it.

I also have a collection of 100,000 business owners to participate in polls. We were mulling over the idea of growing financial planning into our business model, so I asked the question if my followers thought that was a good idea, 70% said yes. Having a social media presence gives me insight into the needs of my clients, and gives a pulse on the broader entrepreneurial community.

People want to do business with a person, not a business. So, we made the decision to promote me, not the business. It helps me get clear on my messaging, but then, it began to take on a life of its own. I never knew I'd be known as "The Morning Guy," for example! That's the way social media can evolve if you allow it to show you the way.

And once you go all in, if you stick with it long enough the impact to your business—from personal experience—can truly be life-altering.

MEASURING RESULTS

Analyze how you currently use social media and the ways you could improve with it.

_____

_____

_____

_____

_____

_____

_____

_____

_____

_____

_____

_____

_____

_____

_____

_____

_____

"Money is only a tool. It will take you wherever you wish, but it will not replace you as the driver."

Ayn Rand

A Professional Accounting Corporation

137

Conclusion

Thank you for taking the time to read my book. Starting out as creative writer and then actually publishing my first book in the business world is something that I never would have believed was in the cards. Regardless, I hope you were able to see behind the curtains of my life and our business. What I am teaching you is exactly what we teach our clients. My hope is that it not only provided you with concrete information about cash flow and business development strategies, but also inspired you to get started on the path to prosperity and success.

If you decide you want to talk further, drop me a DM on Instagram (@tylermcbroom), and we can arrange a talk. I can personally show you how joining our family of clients will save you thousands on your taxes and increase your bottom line.

I'll leave you with one of my favorite Walt Disney quotes, *"All our dreams can come true, if we have the courage to pursue them."*

Life is too short to stay in one spot. Keep pursuing your dreams, Taxsavers.

Made in the USA
Monee, IL
14 February 2021